Survive Life And Live It Up!

Annette Zoheret

I dedicate this book to all of you who are on the journey of self-discovery. May you find health, wealth, peace, joy, and love in your life.

CONTENTS

"A positive attitude may not solve all your problems, but it will annoy enough people to make it worth the effort."

(Herm Albright, 1876 – 1944)

Introduction

There are many self-help books that line the shelves these days. Have you ever wondered why? What is it about our lives that makes us lose touch with ourselves, leaving us burnt out and feeling empty? What is it that we have lost, and how do we get it back? How can we not only survive but actually enjoy ourselves without overeating, drinking, gambling, drowning in debt, or drugging ourselves into oblivion?

Well, stay tuned. This book is deceptively small, but to the point. You don't need a big, fat book, just a few simple truths. The path to inner happiness is not nearly as complex as you may think. Hopefully, this book will help to answer your questions and give you a new start on life, one filled with health, joy, and inner peace.

Your Inner Voice

Let's start by talking about that other person living inside your head— the one who is constantly yammering at you. You may be hearing this voice all the time, but have you ever truly listened? What is it saying to you? It's the root of all evil because that little voice continuously feeds you negative ideas.

When you look into a mirror, you can count on your vocal friend to point out that wrinkled forehead or that pimple growing on your chin. When you step on the scale, there it is again, mentioning that perhaps dessert last night was a mistake. Try on a bathing suit, and you can count on it to criticize the rolls of fat you're attempting to hide by "sucking it in." By now, you sound like a fat, wrinkled, middle-aged teenager suffering from acne.

In fact, that voice makes us all sound like perpetual losers! And since we're prepared to accept criticism much more easily than praise, we've become quite comfortable with running ourselves down. That negative inner voice fills us with fear and doubt about our abilities.

I used to be afraid to parallel park my van, because I was worried about what others would think while watching me fail. Notice that I simply assumed I would fail and be criticized.

How did we get to this point? Some theories claim that we speak to ourselves the way our parents spoke to us, so when I raised my own family, I made sure to praise my children at every opportunity. Yet they still found a way to hear a voice hissing nasty things in their ears.

So, what do we do? How do we banish this evil little voice?
We listen to it very closely, and every time that voice says something negative, we consciously rephrase it and turn it into a positive thought.
"I try" becomes "I do".
"I can't" becomes "I can".
You get the picture.
This may sound easy, but remember it took years to get to where you are, so this will take some effort.

When we were young, learning how to walk took conscious effort, but once we had the skill mastered, the knowledge shifted from our conscious mind to our subconscious. Now we can walk and talk at the same time without tripping over our own feet—at least for most of the time.

Similarly, our negative thinking has been hardwired into our subconscious, so now it requires conscious effort to turn every thought around and make it a positive one. The good news is that once we do this with an iron will and persistence, that inner voice gives up with surprising speed and starts feeding us positive thoughts.

Not only can I walk and talk now that I'm free of the fear of criticism, but my parallel parking skills are second to none!

Exercise #1:

Stand in front of a mirror and look at your face. Take note of what you're thinking and what your inner voice is saying to you. Get into the habit of listening to your own thoughts. Choose a specific attribute you really like about yourself and compliment it. Perhaps you love the colour of your eyes or the shape of your cheekbones. Whatever it is, find it, and concentrate on it. Ignore anything that inspires your little voice to criticize.

From now on, every time you look into the mirror, compliment yourself on how good you look, how smart you are, how well you handle yourself, etc. Every day, find new things about yourself to compliment. Love your body and the being you are.

This will feel uncomfortable and awkward in the beginning. Persevere! This is the biggest hurdle you'll have to take: the idea that you are worthy – worthy of praise, worthy of happiness, worthy of good health, worthy of wealth, and most of all, worthy of love. You are worthy of treating yourself better!

When this idea takes root, you'll immediately notice when you engage in negative thinking. The more often you convert a negative thought into a positive one, the easier it will become. And here's the best part: As your outlook on life improves, so does life itself!

The Power of Beauty

To help you shift from negative to positive, you may have to make a few lifestyle adjustments along with your mental transformation. Many of you are likely in the habit of listening to the radio in the morning. This means that before you've finished your second cup of coffee, you've already heard about theft, rape, murder, and war. Much like watching the evening news—you go to bed with images of fires, screaming sirens, tear- streaked faces, and global mayhem.

Whenever I suggest to people that they stop watching the news, their reaction is one of near panic.
"I won't know what's going on in the world!"
First of all, you know only a fraction of what's going on in the world because there's a lot more going on that you don't hear about. Someone out there decides what makes a good story, and that's the one you get to hear. Everything else never makes prime time.
Secondly, how is your worrying going to help the world?

I quit the news years ago. At first, my co-workers were incredulous when discussing a news item that I wasn't aware of. Now they all know that "Annette doesn't do news" and fill me in when I ask them to. Hearing it without seeing the graphic details allows me to stay in a positive mental state.

The same holds true for watching violent movies and TV shows. Since monitoring what I watch, I've become much more sensitive to violence and find it deeply disturbing. The quality of my sleep has improved dramatically in its absence.

When I listen to music, I try to stay with upbeat lyrics and sound, or classical music. I find harp and violin especially soothing, and I feel the same way about books and pictures. Whenever possible, I surround myself with things that bring me peace of mind.

There is a quote I came across by the nineteenth-century designer, William Morris:

"Have nothing in your house that you do not know to be useful or believe to be beautiful."

That brings us to the topic of clutter. If a messy and dirty home is a thing of beauty to you, then you're a rare individual. Don't get me wrong—I'm not advocating that you spend your few precious hours at home obsessing over your house, but if you find yourself always searching for things, it's time to unclutter. If you look around and feel frustrated, it's time to clean up.

The hard part is in learning not to feel overwhelmed. Remember: it took many years to accumulate all this stuff, so take your time. Choose one corner of one room and just start.

Pick up something and ask yourself: "Is it useful, beautiful, or loved?" If it's none of these things to you, it's time to give it away to an organization where someone else can find it and love it. You'll be amazed by how liberating it is to lose that extra baggage. Clean up one room, and then spend time in it. How do you feel? Does it feel good to be in an open and organized space? Now, when you look for something, everything has its place and you can find it easily.

If you're blessed with a family who sabotages your efforts, you have a better chance of controlling your space if it's orderly to begin with. As a result, you spend less time searching for stuff and are surrounded by a clean and organized space that helps to keep your mind calm and your thoughts organized. This is especially important in the beginning as you make that shift from negative to positive.

The Attitude of Gratitude

Advertising constantly bombards us with what we "need." We are surrounded by billboards and commercials showing us the latest and greatest, convincing us that without it, we are less than the next man or woman. In most cases, our children are worse off than we are. As adults we can at least rationalize, but they tend to believe everything they see and hear and are continuously subjected to tempting offers and peer pressure.

No wonder we live in a society of *have-nots* rather than one of *haves*.

How do we turn this around so that we feel rich even if we're not millionaires? Easily—by looking at what we have rather than what we don't have. This might well sound very strange to you, but here is how you start.

Exercise #2:

Every time you take a hot shower, thank the water for warming and cleansing you.

Every time you eat, thank the food for giving your body strength.

Every time you climb into bed at night, say thank-you for a soft bed and a roof over your head that keeps you warm and dry.

Thank your car for taking you safely to your destination.

Once you get started, you'll be surprised by how many things you can find to be thankful for. The more you concentrate on the wonderful things you have, the more good things come your way while your desire for more decreases.

I came across a quote that illustrates this phenomenon:

"…a basic law:
the more you practice the art of thankfulness,
the more you have to be thankful for.
This, of course, is a fact.
Thankfulness does tend to reproduce in kind.

The attitude of gratitude revitalizes the entire mental process by activating all other attitudes, thus stimulating creativity."

– Norman Vincent Peale, American Pastor,
Author, 1898-1993

Note that Norman lived to the ripe old age of 95, so he must have been doing something right.

Everyone goes on autopilot while eating, showering, driving, or walking. But when you give thanks to the things around you, you're transported into the present and start paying attention to what you're doing right now. For example, you'll start tasting food more intensely, rather than absentmindedly wolfing it down while thinking about a meeting at work or any of the other thousand things that rush through your mind.

Being in the moment and using your senses to experience the present is a powerful tool to quiet the mind and keep stress at bay. Another positive side effect of the attitude of gratitude is that your emotional state changes while you're busy being grateful. Have you ever tried being angry or depressed while feeling grateful? It can't be done! Go ahead and give it a try. It's like patting your head and rubbing your stomach.

We have long been told that forgiveness is important to our health. Holding on to old hurts dams the flow of emotions and eventually makes us sick. For a long time, I couldn't figure out how to forgive. There was no formula for me to use. How do you forgive and move on?

You may be surprised to discover that once you're no longer angry, you can start letting go and begin to forgive—both yourself and others. It happens quite miraculously as you practice the attitude of gratitude. The simple act of forgiveness is incredibly liberating!

Feeling Rich

Feeling rich doesn't automatically mean being rich, although one should follow the other. If bills are weighing you down and you feel like you're financially drowning, then this chapter is for you.

Imagine you're at the grocery store and the person in front of you gets ready to pay a $150 bill. You catch a glimpse of the wallet and see that it's tightly packed with 20 dollar bills. What's the first thought that goes through your mind? Mine would be: "Wow—that person must be rich!" How do you feel about the person? Are you jealous and resentful, or do you think: "Good for you!" Now imagine that you're that person and your friends see you with the same wallet full of cash.

Do you feel a bit guilty?

Do you feel that you owe an explanation or somehow belittle the fact that you're rich?

If you do, you're not alone. You probably grew up in a household where money was scarce and you heard words like "money isn't everything" or "money can't buy you happiness." How about the expression "filthy rich"? I hope you see where I'm headed.

I'm not advocating that money is everything, or that money can make you happy, but money is something that everyone needs, and it's how you use it that makes it good or bad. There is an excellent book entitled *Secrets of the Millionaire Mind* by T. Harv Eker. He goes through great lengths explaining the origins of our financial path, and how we can change it for the better.

The problem is that your view on money is deeply entrenched within your subconscious mind. If you grew up with little money, and you still feel the pinch, how can you possibly begin to feel rich in order to turn the financial tide your way? It's so much easier said than done, but there *is* a way.

YOU become that rich person in the grocery line.
YOU carry a pile of cash!

To some degree, we're all impulse shoppers, and in our defense, it's hard to stick to a budget when we're tempted 24/7. Especially nowadays, with most transactions on debit and credit cards, it's harder than ever to keep a running balance in your head. You think you know how much you've spent; then you receive your monthly credit card bill and nearly faint!

A few years ago, while sitting in my doctor's office, I picked up a family magazine containing an article on finance. I had been managing my family's finances for years and believed I was doing a decent job, but whichever way I played with the figures, I was mystified every month when the bank account was in overdraft, and my budget claimed I should have money left over. The article suggested going back to basics, namely, carrying cash.

Unlike debit or credit cards, when you carry cash, you see it dwindle. You become more aware of how much is left and automatically cut down on impulse shopping. When you have only $10 left, and your choice is to buy milk for the family or a magazine at the checkout, chances are the milk wins out.

Congratulations—you just saved yourself six bucks!

I decided to give this approach a try and guess what? I saved myself hundreds of dollars every month, and my budget actually started to agree with my spending. Another thing that happened is that I *did* start feeling rich. Every time I opened my wallet and saw all that cash, I felt rich. My focus shifted from having debt to having money. Miraculously, as my perception changed, so did my financial situation—and for the better!

The Breath of Life

One of the best things you can do for your body is breathe. Observe how you're sitting or, perhaps, lying down right now. Are you slouching and compressing your chest and your inner organs along with your lungs? Most of us are unaware that we're incapable of taking deep, cleansing breaths because we're hunched over. The result is that we take small, shallow breaths that are not as effective in transporting oxygen to our organs. Deep breathing helps us connect to our body. Go ahead and give it a try. Straighten up and take a deep breath, filling your lungs to capacity. Feel your rib cage expand and your stomach push out. Concentrate on your body while slowly breathing in and out. Listen to your breath.

Take another—it's free.

Just now, while you were busy paying attention to your breathing, were you present in the moment, or were you mentally somewhere else, perhaps composing an e-mail? If you were really concentrating on feeling and hearing your breath, then you were fully present inside your body, and your mind was quiet. It's a wonderful side effect of deep breathing—shutting down your constant stream of thoughts.

Remind yourself several times a day to stop what you're doing, straighten up, and breathe deeply to clear your mind. This is a great tool in stress reduction, and we can take it a step further:

Exercise #3:

I like to do this first thing in the morning, but it also works great during the day or in the evening. If you need to de-stress at work, find yourself an empty washroom cubicle.

Stand up straight, placing your feet hip width apart.
Close your eyes and turn your face towards the light.
(I like sunlight best, but you can always pretend …)
Breathe in deeply, bathing in the golden light of the sun.
(Remember: your eyes are closed.)
Feel your breath.
Hear your breath.
Be fully present in your body.

With every breath, let the golden light enter your body and fill you with peace and love. When you exhale, imagine breathing out grey mist representing your stress and other negative emotions. Let your mind mimic your body. Breathe in oxygen and light; breathe out carbon dioxide and emotional waste. Eventually, when you breathe out, imagine your breath becoming clear, or better yet, golden, which means all negativity has left you. You are now filled with peace and love. This way, you're not only cleansing your body, but also detoxing your mind. Once you've done this several times, you may be able to take a few cleansing breaths at work and feel that same calming effect without locking yourself in a washroom cubicle. This exercise helps you condition your mind and body to relax on command with every deep breath you take. It's a powerful and healthy way to deal with stress.

Food For Thought

On the subject of stress, let's talk about your body and the effect of stress. Chances are good that with successful stress reduction, you may notice a reduction in your waistline as well. During periods of high stress, our bodies release cortisol, adrenaline, and norepinephrine, three major stress hormones. These hormones cause body fat to accumulate around our midsection. Cortisol, the main stress hormone, also increases blood sugar, alters the immune system, and suppresses the digestive and reproductive systems. Long-term, elevated stress levels can lead to heart disease, sleep and digestive problems, depression, obesity, memory impairment, chronic fatigue, and the worsening of skin conditions such as eczema.

Luckily, there are numerous ways to reduce stress and its effects on the body. One we already have talked about is"the breath of life". Another is physical exercise. This doesn't mean you need to run to the gym every day, although spending some time there would definitely be a good idea. A daily walk is sufficient and highly beneficial, especially if you have the chance to do so in nature.

The third is sleep. As adults, we need about seven to eight hours of sleep each night. Most of us get far less. Chronic sleep deprivation has a devastating effect on overall health and mental ability. During periods of high stress, many of us either can't get to sleep or wake up at 3 a.m. with all kind of thoughts racing through our head.

There are a number of ways that can help you get the sleep you need. If you want to stay with a drug-free method, try a cup of hot milk with honey, a soak in a hot bath with Epsom salts, or sleep-enhancing music. You can also try a dose of melatonin, the body's natural sleep hormone, but as with all medication, exercise caution and consult your physician. If you're one of those lucky individuals with a flexible schedule, allow yourself the luxury of a power nap. Studies have shown that a twenty-minute nap is optimal for enhancing cognitive function and increasing your energy level.

A fourth way to reduce stress is through nutrition. There are some wonderful books dedicated to this subject, and I've included two book titles in the reference section at the back. For me, the journey to good nutrition began with a couple of documentaries on Netflix: *Food Matters* and *Hungry for Change*. If you're used to eating processed foods, it will take a while to learn what to do with "real" food. However, if you've ever had your teenager look at a loaded fridge and complain that there's nothing to eat, you know you're on the right track!

In general, it's best to eat foods with minimal processing whenever possible and include protein in every meal. Most important, read labels! Manufacturers include significant amounts of sugar and salt in almost everything. There is no distinction between added sugar and naturally occurring sugar. At most, the label will read "unsweetened" or "no sugar added." Here is an example of what I previously considered healthy:

One bowl of granola with bran buds, flax, and hemp seeds, mixed with half a cup of fresh berries, and a low-fat mini-yogurt.

Unbeknownst to me, I was consuming a whopping five teaspoons of sugar, some of it naturally occurring and some of it added. Naturally occurring sugars are much healthier than added sugars, such as high fructose corn syrup. The labelling tends to be misleading, because the consumer's attention is drawn to the bold print stating "contains whole grain," "fat free," or "excellent source of calcium," while the sugar content is in small print on the back of the product.

Stay away from anything that claims to be "naturally sweetened with sucralose." There is nothing natural about it, since it's a modified chlorine molecule. The reason sucralose, also known as Splenda, has no calories, is because your body cannot break it down and unlike aspartame absorbs only a minimal amount. This is why it is considered safer than aspartame. Even though individual manufacturers use what has been defined as safe amounts of aspartame, if you frequently add it to your hot beverage and consume several cans of artificially sweetened pop a day, you may well be consuming more than what is considered safe.

Therefore, consider using natural sweeteners, such as maple syrup or honey. Make sure it's local honey from within 50 km. of your home. Personally, I've had great success in reducing my environmental allergies by using a teaspoon of honey in my morning coffee.

If you want to bake and need something with the consistency of sugar, consider maple sugar, or crystalized cane juice. The cane juice has not been superheated so still contains the enzymes that help your body balance its sugar level.

In order to maintain a consistent blood glucose level, you need to eat approximately every three hours, especially if you want to lose weight. While this sounds counterintuitive, there is an underlying rationale: If you let your blood sugar level drop to the point where you're hungry, it will spike when you eat. Your body will use only what it needs at the moment, and the rest is stored as fat— yup, around your middle! If you want to lose weight, avoid the glucose roller-coaster.

Juicing is another great way to maintain good health or lose weight. This is especially handy if you have young children who won't eat their broccoli. To choose a good juicer, go online and do your research. It can be

daunting—I ended up buying an expensive juicer with the most positive reviews. So far, I have yet to regret spending the money. This was the first winter without a single cold or sniffle,
I have more energy and a healthy glow.

Here's my favourite juice recipe:
    4 leaves of kale
    1 cucumber
    2 Granny Smith apples
    1 lemon
    2 oranges
    2 large or 3 medium-sized carrots
    2 mid-sized beets
    (Optional: pears, grapes, berries, pineapple or anything else you can think of.)

I make this juice before cooking dinner to satisfy my immediate hunger and to make it easier not to overeat at night. For weight loss, you can replace one meal a day with juice alone. This recipe makes enough for two glasses at night and two the next morning.

And finally—our body *needs* vitamins C and D. In North America, pretty much everyone is Vitamin-D deficient. If you are under the age of 50, you should take about 1,000 IU in the winter and 500 IU in the summer. If you are over 50 you should double that dose to help avoid osteoporosis. The reason you need a lower dose in summer is because your body manufactures Vitamin D when exposed to sunshine.

Your body's cells are renewed continuously by using the nutrition you provide. While red blood cells live for about four months, skin cells live for approximately three to four weeks. Imagine what a difference you could make in a relatively short time!

It Is What It Is

Would you agree with me if I said "The past is gone and you cannot change it"? How about "The future is unknown and you have no control over it"? Did you know that 99% of stress comes from worrying about the past or fretting about the future?

"If only I had …"

"What if …?"

If we have no control over the past or the future, that leaves us with the present. Even in the "here and now," our power is limited. We can't dictate what others should do, or how events should unfold, but we do have complete control over ourselves. We determine what we do right now, how we react, and what we think.

Since the present becomes the past, it stands to reason that where we are in life right now is a direct result of our past actions. This is a hard pill to swallow for some of us because it means that we can no longer blame others for our misfortune. Our parents are not at fault, nor is our boss, our partner, our children, or anyone else. Even though some of us may have had some extremely unfortunate events in our past, the decision on how to deal with our misfortune was ours alone.

A few years ago, my cousin, a brilliant surgeon and father of three, locked himself in his office on a Friday evening and gave himself a lethal injection. He had been suffering from depression, and even though he had planned to go on vacation with his family the next day, he suddenly saw no way out and decided to end his life.

Our entire family was devastated, especially my uncle. This was not the first blow he had received. A few years earlier, his wife, whom he had nursed for many years, died as a result of rheumatoid arthritis. Yet, he never appeared angry or upset and always had a smile or a kind word. Whenever the family got together, the conversation always revolved around the same questions:

Why didn't my cousin seek help?

How could he leave his children?

He could have just taken some time off, etc.

I noticed that my uncle became very quiet on these occasions.

"How are you coping?" I asked him one day.

He sighed and said: "It was my son's decision, and the quicker I can accept that, the better it will be for me."

My uncle lived by the philosophy of "It is what it is." Even though he had great hardship in his life, he also had great joy. He was a genuinely happy man who lived far into his nineties.

As soon as you come to realize that you're not a victim of others' wrongdoings, and that you're in control, you discover that you're immensely powerful.

I finally understood this while sitting in a plane on the tarmac, along with a few hundred other people, waiting for the arrival of a delayed passenger. By the time the individual made an appearance, five other passengers had decided they wanted to leave the plane since they had already missed their connection. We were obliged to wait another twenty minutes while airport staff removed their luggage from the bowels of the plane. Meanwhile, I could feel myself getting increasingly tense, worried, and angry, as were many other passengers. The atmosphere of unrest in the plane was palpable. Suddenly, an old saying popped into my mind:

> *God, grant me the serenity to accept the things I cannot change,*
> *The courage to change the things I can,*
> *And the wisdom to know the difference.*
> (based on the original version attributed to Reinhold Niebuhr, US Protestant theologian, 1892 – 1971)

This is an amazingly powerful philosophy. Instead of wasting our energies getting upset over events beyond our control, we can choose to accept what we can't change, and when the time comes for us to shine, we have the courage to do whatever must be done.

"Is this something you can change?" I asked myself.

The answer was "No, not really."

"So what is gained by getting upset?"

"Nothing."

"Well then, sit back and relax!"

As soon as I had come to this conclusion, I felt much better. I took a deep breath and immediately felt better, all anger and tension melting away. Instead of feeling victimized by events beyond my control, I suddenly felt powerful and in charge. I had acted by making a decision. Nothing else had changed, only my perception. Now, every time there is a decision to be made, I ask myself: "Is it something you can change?"

By picking your battles wisely, you become much more effective when deciding to take action. If you happen to be a fan of *Harry Potter*, you may remember the wise words of Professor Dumbledore: "It is our choices...that show what we truly are, far more than our abilities." And if you don't think that only one person's choices can make a difference, think of Hitler and Ghandi.

Daily Mantra

Here is a hodgepodge of tricks to include in your emotional toolkit. Try them out and then pick and choose what works for you. In the end, it's best to develop your own coping strategies and mantras, but here is one to help you on your way.

This mantra is similar to "the breath of life," only this time, as you breathe in, sweep your arms up over your head and back down as you breathe out. With every breath, turn your torso slightly, once to the left and once to the right, so that your arms come up at ten o'clock, two o'clock, etc. What you're doing is creating a sphere of energy around your body by sweeping your arms over your head and down in different positions around your body. In addition, while you're breathing and sweeping your arms, think of, or say, positive affirmations.

Exercise #4:

Stand with feet hip width apart, close your eyes, and turn your face to the light.

Speak or think the words as you move:

Sweep arms up while breathing in. *I am safe.*

Sweep arms down and breathe out. *And I am protected.*

Turn your torso to the right.

Sweep arms up and breathe in. *I love…*

Sweep arms down and breathe out. *…and I am loved.*

Return to centre.

Sweep arms up and breathe in. *I am healthy and strong…*

Sweep arms down and breathe out. *…I am full of energy.*

Turn torso to the left:

Sweep arms up and breathe in. *I am wise…*

Sweep arms down and breathe out: *…and my decisions are good.*

Return to centre.

Sweep arms up and breathe in. *I am successful…*

Sweep arms down and breathe out. *…Everything I touch turns to gold.*

End by placing your hands over your chest, bow your head, and speak/think these words: *Thank you* (insert God, Creator, Universe, or whatever your belief is) *for the divine spark within me.*
Everything I need will appear when I need it.

Right here, right now, at this very moment, all is well.
Repeat *thank you* as often as you like.

Envision yourself surrounded by a bubble of positive energy that protects you from anything negative, including the common cold. This is the basic version. You can add to this mantra, and change it in response to your needs and feelings of the moment. This mantra is very powerful and has seen me through dark times. It has allowed me to sleep well at night and continue to function at work when my world at home was falling apart.

The other positive side effect shown is that by sweeping your arms up and down, you give your body a good stretch. Recent studies have discovered that standing in a "power pose" of legs apart and arms stretched up and out, you actually reduce excess levels of cortisol and increase your testosterone in as little as two minutes! Assuming the "power pose" in an elevator or washroom before going into a stressful situation, such as a job interview, adjusts your body language, and along with it your mental outlook, so that you come across less nervous and more confident.

No matter what happens in your life, stand tall and keep reminding yourself that *all is well.* If you repeat "All is well" over and over, it will be!
Remember: your perception makes the difference!

Decision Making and Crisis Mode

Sometimes, we're faced with life-altering decisions that can drive us to distraction. "Should I or shouldn't I?" is a questions that's with us day and night. We know that whatever decision we make, it could well affect the rest of our lives.

Sometimes, we already know the answer but are unaware that we do. If you've been doing the exercises so far, then you've learned to connect with, and listen to, your body.
Sit back, relax, and breathe deeply.
Hear and feel your breath.
Empty your mind.
Envision yourself one year into the future and already living with your decision.
How did your body react?
There is a reason for the expression "I had a gut feeling."
Did you feel your stomach clench or back muscles tighten?
Maybe your reaction was much more powerful, like a strong revulsion. If you didn't feel much of anything, try again, this time choosing your other option.
What happened this time?
Often times, your body can tell you what your decision should be. Deep inside, you already have the answer. Always be true to yourself.

Let's imagine you've made your decision but have no idea how to get there from here. Financially, it appears impossible, the likelihood of all the pieces falling into place astronomical, and the obstacles insurmountable.

Remember your mantra: Everything I need will appear when I need it.

It helps when you're very clear about what it is you need. Write it down and read it daily. Your thoughts are energy and have a powerful influence on the physical world. By clearly stating your goal, writing it down, and repeating it, you're sending vibrations into the universe to attract what you're asking for.

> "Whatever the mind can conceive and believe, it can achieve."
>
> *(Napoleon Hill*, October 26, 1883 –
> November 8, 1970)

For example, if you need a new place to live, or a job, describe it in detail. However, mere thoughts are not enough. To succeed, you must also act. When I went through my separation, we had sold our house, and I was looking for a new home. It seemed impossible that I would find a house to fit my needs as well as my budget. With three daughters, I looked for a place with four bedrooms and two bathrooms. But I also had two huge dogs with a litter of puppies on the way, and so I also needed a large yard. I made a list, and since I love fireplaces, I threw that into the bargain. I moved heaven and earth to employ the universal law of attraction or whatever you choose to call it. I looked at my list and read it out loud.

My logical mind screamed: "There is no way!"

I "windmilled" my arms and repeated my mantra every time I felt despair creeping in. When my mind started racing, I began breathing and mentally chanting, *Right here, right now, at this very moment, all is well,* pushing away all other thoughts. I worked hard to keep my sanity and appear calm to my family and the outside world. What if the closing date came and I had no place to go? Time was slipping away and there was still no house. I searched the Internet and drove through neighbourhoods. With every house I visited, my heart sank a little more. There was too much on my list. There was no way.

And then, one Sunday morning, when I logged into my computer to search once again, I thought: *Today, I will find my house.*

And I did.

The universe outdid itself. It gave me a home with four bedrooms, two bathrooms, and a huge yard. Not only did it grant me a fireplace, it gave me two! And it remembered that I always wanted a screened-in porch. As unbelievable as it seems, somehow the money also appeared when I needed it, and in the end, I managed to reduce my debt rather than adding to it.

What I'm saying is, never give up, no matter how impossible it seems.

Persevere—and you will get there!

Loss and Grieving

There inevitably comes a time in our life when we experience loss. It can come in any form: the loss of a loved one, a pet, a job, a dream, a miscarriage, a major disappointment—all these situations cause grief.

Sometimes, we don't even know that when we feel sad, we're actually grieving the loss of something. I usually have to sit back and analyze my feelings before realizing that I'm not having some random attack of sadness, but that I *am* actually grieving.

Dr. Christine Northrup, a well-known holistic medical practitioner, describes emotions being like a river. If you don't let them run through you, the river dams and the waters stagnate. Over time, bottled-up emotions will lead to all sorts of health problems.

It's all right to feel sad or angry sometimes. Be aware, though, that there's likely a reason, even if you can't figure it out right away. However, do yourself, and others, the courtesy of an explanation. "I'm feeling upset today. Please don't take it personally." In that way, your family or friends know that if you don't respond with enthusiasm to one of their ingenious ideas, it's because you're working through some emotions, and that's OK—you're entitled.

I attended a funeral recently where the minister described grief as a Lazy Susan in a kitchen. Every time we open the cupboard, we're served a new emotion: anger, sadness, disbelief, more anger, a bit of joy in between, and down again. If we allow for our emotions to run through us like a river, identifying the cause whenever possible, we will find that we can get past the negative more quickly and return to a positive state of mind.

Detach With Love

Let's assume that you've practiced the exercises in this book on a daily basis for a year. You have changed. You cannot love and respect your body and continue to abuse it.

If you've been practicing "the attitude of gratitude," then you've been at the receiving end of many wonderful experiences. You've learned to listen to your body and recognize when it's stressed. Using "the breath of life", you've reduced that stress, and most of the time, you're feeling at peace yet energized.

Your health has improved drastically. You have been eating a healthy diet, and as a result, your weight most likely has adjusted to what it should be. Your daily mantra is keeping you grounded and in control. Your posture has most likely improved with the frequent use of the "power pose."

Naturally, your next step is the desire to pass along your knowledge. You're feeling great, and you want your loved ones to share in your good fortune. Unfortunately, it doesn't work that way. It's as if you can see something that others are blind to. Imagine that you're walking along dropping a trail of bread crumbs. It's up to those walking with you to pick up the crumbs. If they choose to ignore them, you must accept that as their choice. Remember: you're the only one under your control.

The best you can do is live by example. Everyone has to find this path of enlightenment on their own. Some will read this book and toss it because it simply doesn't resonate with them. Perhaps another book will. The point is that they must be ready to receive this information. Since you can't force people to see the light, what *can* you do? You can detach with love. You're not responsible for anyone's actions but your own. We all have choices and it's up to us to make the right ones for ourselves.

As you love and respect yourself, you'll find that you treat others with the same love and respect. As your own needs are met, you begin to focus on helping others. You'll live to enrich the lives of others, and in the process, you'll rediscover the ancient adage:

"It is in giving that we receive." (St. Francis of Assisi)

When out and about during the day, thank and bless the people you come into contact with—the waiter who serves your lunch, the server who pours your coffee, colleagues at work, and so on. If it seems awkward at first, just remember that whenever you say, "Have a great day!" that is, in effect, what you're already doing.

And Finally ...

… something about myself.

I was born in Stuttgart, Germany, into a neighbourhood of doctors, lawyers, and wealthy businessmen. My father was a pharmacist and my mother a housewife whose job it was to supervise the nanny, the maid, and the cleaning lady. Everything was a routine in our home. Each day Mom went to the market to purchase fresh ingredients for my father's hot mid-day meal. The house was cleaned daily, the silver polished weekly, and the windows washed monthly.

Life fell apart suddenly when my father died of a heart attack. I was just seven years old. He didn't believe in life insurance and left my mother with a formidable pile of debt, a business she was not legally allowed to operate, two young girls, and the family dog. Gone were the nanny, the maid, and the cleaning lady.

On the advice of our family physician, who felt that we children needed to recuperate, my sister and I were shipped off to an expensive children's home in the Black Forest, which was paid for by the government health insurance program. This was arranged to give my mother time to put the family affairs in order. The home came highly recommended, and I'm sure nobody was aware or would believe what methods were used to nurse ailing children back to health. Weight gain was achieved by feeding kids until they vomited and then forcing them to eat what they had expelled.

Every morning we were lined up naked to run through a freezing shower while we all counted to three. That was the measure of time we were meant to stay in the shower. Soap was not involved until the end of six weeks, when we were given a hot bath and had our hair washed. It felt like luxury beyond our wildest dreams, and we couldn't believe our luck. The next day, our mother arrived to pick us up. We were rosy cheeked, smelling like flowers, and appeared to be the picture of health. She didn't believe a word we told her to the contrary.

Six months later, we boarded a plane and flew to Canada to live on my uncle's farm. He raised Great Danes and horses. For a timid child from the city, this new world, with its Jurassic Park-sized animals and its strange language, did nothing for self-confidence. Don't get me wrong—I loved the farm and having my own Shetland pony, although it was Pitchenini's heart's desire to get me off his back as soon as I got on. We had no saddle and made our own bridle, and we had more adventures than I could ever recount here. I know I'm not doing my life story justice here, but I promise I will soon. As you read this, I'm busy writing my memoirs.

We stayed in Canada for one year before returning to Germany. By now, I no longer spoke German correctly, nor did I speak perfect English. Instead, it was a strange mixture of both, which led me to believe that I would be stuck in third grade for the rest of my life. I was on my second repetition, and I was already nine years old.

Add to that the fact that I was cursed with an abnormally large nose, and you had the perfect reasons for my classmates to bully, pursue, insult, beat up, and alienate me at every opportunity they got. For two years, I was followed home by the same four girls who made it their life's purpose to make mine miserable. They went so far as to recruit others to get close to me on the pretense of friendship, only to betray, and ultimately, deliver me to them. This was not a happy time. I was homesick for the farm animals and my friends in Canada.

At twelve years old, I was involved in a serious car crash that left my mother with a broken nose and fractured skull. In the years that followed, death took both my grandmothers, my grandfather, my brother from my father's first marriage, and finally, my three-year-old cousin. By the time I was seventeen years old, I firmly believed that if I had a good time, it would soon be followed by punishment—someone dear would be taken from me. I lived in constant fear of losing my mother, or someone else close to me, and I was running out of relatives at an alarming rate. As a result, I suffered bouts of severe depression.

Life picked up in my twenties. I had a successful career in information technology as a programmer/analyst, a husband, three daughters, and a large century-old home in the country. Even though I appeared to have it all, I lived with constant stress and worry. My husband had a tendency not to call home when running late, which he did frequently. In my mind, he met with at least one fatal accident every week. Finances were a constant source of concern, as was my children's safety.

Finally, at one of my regular checkups, my dentist noticed the inside of my cheeks, bitten raw at night.
"Annette, the light has gone from your eyes," she said.
"If you keep up this level of stress, you'll put yourself into the hospital."
She sent me to a physiotherapist who assessed my constant back pain and prescribed a large exercise ball that I should use instead of my office chair. At the same time, a friend lent me a book entitled *Talking to Heaven* and put me in touch with a native shaman who came for a visit to cleanse our house.

The reason for this was that the home we lived in was also occupied by another tenant—one who couldn't be seen, but who enjoyed playing with our chandelier lights and hiding various items all over the house, like the bottle opener that mysteriously travelled from the kitchen drawer into the upstairs bedroom and reappeared in my jewelry box!

The shaman, White Eagle, told me that there was a family of spirits in the house.

"Do not fear them," he said.

"They are here to protect the house and its inhabitants."

However, he felt that they had experienced pain here and were trapped by it. We traipsed through the house, smudging and blessing each room, until White Eagle declared the job done and the house free of negative energy.

During the following days, I felt as if someone had lifted a weight off my chest and had opened all the windows to let in fresh air. The children, usually fighting and arguing, played peacefully together. My husband, often moody and introverted, talked and laughed with them. The entire house felt like it was bathed in sunshine.

Then it happened—I woke up in the middle of the night to the smell of roses, and in my mind I saw a young woman in a long, lilac-coloured dress. She had a kind, serious face, and I knew she had lost a child.

"All is well," she told me, "now that Victoria is here."

"Are you of the light?" I asked, as taught in *Talking to Heaven.*

The answer came in another gentle wave of floral scent. I sat bolt upright in bed and discovered that my nose was completely plugged with seasonal allergies. There was no way I should have been able to smell anything!

The next night I was awakened again—this time by a child's voice whispering into my ear, but I was unable to understand the sound of baby talk. On the third night, I instinctively felt the strong presence of a male spirit. Somehow the shaman had opened a door that I previously had toyed with on occasion, but had shut and locked again.

The next day, as my husband and I were standing no more than a foot apart, enjoying a freshly brewed cup of coffee, Victoria returned and made her presence known by her distinctive floral scent. It was so strong that I felt like I was drowning in it, but there was something else—a message of thank-you, and suddenly, I was bathed in an unearthly joy that I can only call a glimpse of heaven. I felt something inside me trying to force its way out and up. All I wanted to do was follow this immense joy and join Victoria. It didn't matter that I had children, a husband, a home, and responsibilities.

My soul remembered heaven!

"Can you smell it?" I asked my husband full of excitement. "Can you feel it?"

"I smell coffee," he said.

I realized that this message had been intended for me alone. The moment that lasted merely seconds changed my life. The constant fear that lived inside me was gone, as was the sorrow for all those I had lost. How could I be sad when I knew they existed in a state of pure joy?

The years that followed were tough ones. I lost my marriage, my home, my mother-in-law, my aunt, my mother, a close girlfriend, but I didn't lose myself. On the contrary, I developed coping strategies to not only help me survive, but to enjoy life despite its hard times.

Henry Kissinger once said:
"A diamond is a chunk of coal made good under pressure."

Chances are, if you've picked up this book, times are tough and you're looking for a way to make it through. You will! And when you emerge on the other side, remember that you are a precious gem and deserve to be treated as such, by yourself and others.

Namaste!

Acknowledgements

I would like to thank my niece, Floriana Ehninger-Cuervo, for her wonderful artwork, as well as my daughter, Maya ter Stege, for her wise counsel and creative cover-design.

My gratitude also goes to my editor, Irene Kavanagh, for her keen eye and discerning comments. Thank you to my family and friends who have laughed and cried with me over the years and encouraged me to share my writing with you.

I would like to thank the following writers for sharing their wisdom through their books:

Louise Hay ~ You Can Heal Your Life
Andrew Matthews ~ *Being Happy*
Rhonda Byrne ~ *The Secret*
Dr. Jonn Matsen, N.D. ~ *Eating Alive*
Monica Reinagel ~ The Inflammation-Free Diet Plan
Richard Gordon ~ Quantum Touch: The Power to Heal
T. Harv Eker. ~ Secrets of the Millionaire Mind

And J.K. Rowling, for allowing me to escape into Harry Potter's world whenever mine becomes much too complicated!